THE
CHOICE

THE ARBINGER INSTITUTE

ORDERING INFORMATION. Copies of *The Choice* can be ordered through the Arbinger Institute. Training that develops and applies the material in the book is also available through Arbinger. For orders or inquiries please contact Arbinger:

The Arbinger Institute
1.801.447.9244
www.arbinger.com

The Choice was originally published in 1998.
Linacre Prince Edition 2014

Contents

VIII The Responsive Way

IX Paths in Psychology

X Choice

❖

INTRODUCTION

A team of scholars associated with the Arbinger Institute has made a discovery that solves an age-old problem at the heart of the human sciences.

Freud noticed that people often are blind to their actual motivations and fail to understand their influence on others. He also noticed that this blindness seems willful or strategic. That is, to an outside observer, it appears that people systematically create their own obstacles to well-being—without knowing they are creating them—and then resist any attempts to overcome those obstacles.

But this creates a paradox. How can one who is blind to the trouble he has created see and resist so perfectly any attempts to correct that trouble? Modern psychology began as an attempt to explain this paradox, a paradox that has become known as *self-deception*.

The personal and organizational implications of self-deception are immense. Recognizing this, scholars working at the deepest levels of the human sciences have attempted to

explain it. Meanwhile, most of the popular psychological de-
bate has continued forward, with the participants and the public
unaware that everything being debated has a problem at its very core.

Finally, a solution to the self-deception problem has been discov-
ered. This little book outlines in an accessible and thought-provoking
way the flow of that discovery.

I
Two Ways

❖

Ways of Being

On the surface, humans differ widely. In our behavior—our
"doings"—we display immense variety.

—m—

But below the surface the world is different.

At the level of who we "are"—our being—there are two ways only.

❖

The Responsive Way

One way of being is to see others as they are—as people.

Seeing them as people, I am *responsive* to their reality—
their concerns, their hopes, their needs, their fears.

Others are as real to me as I am to myself.

—∿—

Seeing others truly, I am true.

❖

The Resistant Way

The other way is to see people as objects.

Seeing them as objects, I am *resistant* to their reality.
If I see others at all, they are less than I am—less relevant,
less important, less real.

Seeing people as less than they are, I am deceived
about their reality.

—∾—

Seeing others falsely, I am false.

❖

Deeper than Behavior

A common misunderstanding:

Being "responsive," my behavior is "soft"; being "resistant,"
my behavior is "hard."

—⁓—

The truth:

Being "responsive" I see others as people; being "resistant,"
I see others as objects.

This distinction is deeper than behavior.

—⁓—

Consider:

Complimenting others, for example, might be considered "soft,"
and correcting others "hard."

But I can compliment or correct another because it will help *them,*
or I can compliment or correct another because it will help *me.*

One way I am seeing a person—I am being responsive.

The other way I am seeing an object—I am being resistant.

I can compliment or correct in either way.

—⚯—

Likewise with almost any behavior.

There are two ways to say "Yes," two ways to say "No,"
two ways to smile, two ways to frown, two ways to discipline,
two ways to reward.

—⚯—

Almost any behavior can be done in either way.

❖

INFLUENCE

But consider how different two apparently identical behaviors can be:

Seeing me as a person, someone compliments me.

Seeing me as an object, someone compliments me.

Do the compliments feel the same to me?

—⁂—

Or consider how different it feels to be corrected by someone who sees me as a person as compared to someone who sees me as an object.

—⁂—

Whatever I "do" on the surface, people respond to who I am being when I am doing it.

—⁂—

Way of being determines influence.

II

The Point of Choice

❖

Self-Betrayal

As a person, I know what it means to be a person.
I have a sense of what people need.

For example: I see a person in need, and feel to help.

—∽—

My responsiveness to others' needs is my deepest sense of
what is right.

I can resist this responsiveness toward others' needs.

If I do, I betray my deepest sense of what is right.

—∽—

Betray my deepest sense of what is right and I betray *myself.*

❖

SELF-JUSTIFICATION

When I betray myself, I begin seeing myself, others, and the world
in ways that justify me.

—∞—

Example: My child cries in the middle of the night, and I have a
desire to get up and tend to her before my spouse wakes up.
But I don't.

I now say:

"I got up last time."
"My spouse is not as busy as I am."
"My spouse is probably feigning sleep."

—∞—

Another example: I obtain information that would help a coworker
and think I should share it. But I don't.

I now say:

"This person doesn't help me."
"This person is too dependent on others already."
"I worked hard for this information."

—∞—

The people I felt to help now seem blameworthy.

I feel justified in *not* helping.

—ᴍ—

But did they seem blameworthy when I felt to help?

Why do they seem blameworthy now?

—ᴍ—

Betray myself and I seek to be justified by blaming others.
I become resistant to them.

❖

People or Objects

Betraying myself, people to help become objects of blame.

—∞—

Instead of people with their own lives, I now see
others as obstacles in mine, or as vehicles to be used
for my purposes, or as irrelevancies that offer
me no advantage.

—∞—

Consider:

When I felt to get up and tend the baby before my spouse woke up,
was my spouse a *person* or an *object* to me?

And how was I seeing my coworker when I felt I should share the
information I had obtained?

—∞—

Compare:

How did I see my spouse and my coworker *after* I betrayed my
sense of what I should do for them?

—∞—

Responsive is who I was.

Resistant is the way I made myself in self-betrayal.

—⁂—

Reducing people to mere objects is the way I resist them.

❖

THE QUESTION

Every moment offers the choice of two ways.

Will I be responsive to others and see them as people, or resistant
to others and see them as objects?

—⚡—

My life consists of moments with others:

My spouse needs my help.

My child needs attention.

My sister needs an apology.

My friend needs a listening ear.

My neighbor needs a helping hand.

My employer needs my commitment.

My coworker needs my assistance.

My assistant needs an encouraging word.

—⚡—

The people in my life—have I done right by them?

What would *they* say my choice has been?

—∿—

The quality of my life will depend on that choice.

III
The Resistant Way

❖

Horribilizing

When I betray myself, I "horribilize" others: I focus on and
exaggerate their faults.

—⁘—

"But," you say, *"others can be horrible. They can do wrong to you."*

Yes.

—⁘—

But when do others appear *most* wrong to me?

The coworker I failed to help: When did his failings seem bigger
to me—before I decided not to share information with him . . .
or afterward?

When did my spouse's failings seem bigger to me—
before I decided not to tend our child . . . or afterward?

—⁘—

In self-betrayal, I seize upon and magnify others' imperfections.

How profitable I find others' faults when I need to justify my own.

❖

Blaming Emotions

Betraying myself, I blame not only with thoughts,
but feelings too.

—⁓—

When I think of the person I failed to help, I may feel resentful,
indifferent, or irritated.

Resentment says: *He has caused me to resent him.*

Indifference says: *Her insignificance has caused me to
disregard her.*

Irritation says: *I am irritated because he is irritating.*

My feelings tell me the *other* made me feel as I do.

—⁓—

But I didn't feel this way when I first felt to help. Why do I feel
this way now?

The reason: I resent the person I failed to help . . . *because* I
failed to help.

—⁓—

So when I betray myself, my emotions become dishonest.
They make a false accusation about their own cause, blaming
something or someone outside myself.

Feeling such feelings, I believe them.

Believing them, I believe their lie.

—◊—

The truth:

I may feel those feelings, but I am not *made* to feel them.

I wasn't feeling them when I felt to help.

❖

Self-Victimization

When I see people to help, I am their friend.

When I see people to blame, I experience myself as their victim.

—⚡—

Betraying myself, help fades to blame.

—⚡—

I make myself into a victim.

❖

Distortion of Values

Violate my deepest sense of right and wrong and I do so *in the name* of right and wrong.

—ϻ—

Betraying myself and blaming others, I see others as forcing me to violate a *value* or *principle*.

I say, *"This person doesn't help me."*

Interesting how important fairness has suddenly become to me.

I say, *"This person is too dependent on others."*

Interesting how important her growth has suddenly become to me.

I say, *"This person is not as busy as I am."*

Interesting how my personal productivity is suddenly so important to me.

—ϻ—

My values and principles are different than they were before betraying myself.

They are different because *I* am different.

—ɯ—

In self-betrayal, values and principles become distorted.
I exploit them—even deform and exaggerate them—so they can
protect me from the truth.

I exploit the right to justify my wrong.

❖

Insistence on Being "Right"

I was not exploiting values or principles when I felt to help.

Why am I exploiting them now?

—∞—

Because:

Do wrong and I need to feel justified.

If I have principle on my side, I feel I am "in the right." And if
I am "in the right," I feel justified.

So do wrong and I exploit values and principles to convince myself
that I am in the right.

—∞—

Interesting that I didn't worry about being "in the right"
when I first felt to help, but only after I failed to help.

If I were right, would I really need to convince myself?

❖

Living a Lie

When I betray myself, my experience becomes radically
transformed.

Good people seem less good, and bad people more bad.

Helping feelings turn to blaming feelings.

Those in need of help become victimizers unworthy of help.

Values become less valued as values, and more
valued as justifications.

The desire to be right *for* another becomes a quest to be
more right *than* the other.

—⟁—

So when I betray myself, I enter a way of being that is inherently
resistant, self-justifying, and false.

—⟁—

I may *think* I am justified.

I may *feel* I am justified.

But betray myself, and I can't trust perception—even my
perception of conscience.

The person I once felt to help, I now feel *shouldn't* be helped.

My thoughts and feelings lie.

—ɯ—

The lie that I am justified is a lie that I *live*.

IV

The Resistant Way and Self

❖

Preoccupation with Self

Who am I thinking of when I am inflating others' faults to
minimize my own?

Who am I thinking of when I am blaming others for how I feel?

Who am I thinking of when I am making myself a victim?

Who am I thinking of when I am exploiting values to
protect myself?

Who am I thinking of when I am convincing myself that
I am right?

—∽—

Compare:

Who was I thinking of when I felt to help?

—∽—

Betray myself and I become consumed with self.

❖

Self-Justifying Images

Betray myself and I present an image of myself.

The image is that I am the undeserving victim of those
I am blaming.

—⁂—

When I betrayed myself in not helping my spouse, I said:

"I got up last time."
"My spouse is not as busy as I am."
"My spouse is probably feigning sleep."

When I betrayed myself in not helping my coworker, I said:

"This person doesn't help me."
"This person is too dependent on others."
"I've worked hard for this information."

—⁂—

These attitudes toward others reveal corresponding attitudes
toward myself:

"I'm the sort of person who is fair."
"I'm the sort of person who is important."
"I'm the sort of person who will not be taken advantage of."

"I'm the sort of person everyone ought to respect."
"I'm the sort of person who is smarter than, and knows
what's best for, others."
"I'm the sort of person who deserves more because I work harder."

—⁂—

To betray myself is to portray myself. It is to portray myself
in ways that justify me.

❖

Self-Image Writ Large

If I repeatedly justify myself in self-betrayal, then such self-justifying images become *characteristic* of me.

—∾—

Consider how such self-justifying images counterfeit the noblest attributes:

"I'm the sort of person who thinks of others."

Isn't it good to think of others?

Yes.

But who am I thinking of when I am thinking of *myself* as the sort of person who thinks of others?

Like all self-justifying images, this one lies. It pretends to be about something noble. But it is really just about me.

How ignoble to *portray* nobility.

—∾—

Other self-justifying images find refuge in the basest attributes:

"I'm the sort of person who is worthless."

How comforting it is to feel that no one can expect anything
of me . . .

and that others are too judgmental and mean to *deserve* anything
from me.

—∿—

Whether they claim my virtue or justify my vice, once characteristic
of me, the self-justifying images I create in self-betrayal keep me
focused on myself.

I come to see others *in terms of* the self-justifying images
I have created.

If their actions *challenge* the claim made by my self-justifying image,
I see them as a threat or obstacle.

If they *reinforce* the claim made by my self-justifying image,
I see them as an ally or vehicle.

If they *fail to matter* to my self-justifying image, I see them as
unimportant or irrelevant.

—∿—

Seeing others in terms of my self-justifying images,

I now enter new situations already seeing others as objects.

I see them *to begin with* in terms of their meaning for my view of myself.

—⟋⟍—

My self-betrayal now is ongoing, and toward people or groups of people in general.

I resent anyone who suggests in word or deed that I am not the kind of person I am portraying myself to be.

—⟋⟍—

How different was my experience when I felt to help.

❖

Self-Deception

Betraying myself, I am wrong.

But betraying myself, my whole experience—my thoughts, my feelings, my self-image—everything convinces me I am right.

I *feel* justified.

—⚬—

This means that when I am betraying and justifying myself, I can't see that I am betraying and justifying myself.

I think I am resisting others because they have mistreated me.

But the truth is: I am resisting others because I have mistreated them.

I am self-deceived.

—⚬—

This is not to say that I am not being mistreated.

But it is to say that others' mistreatment of me is not why I am resisting them.

There is a way to see others as people even when they are doing wrong.

To see them as objects is something that *I* am doing.

—ɷ—

Betray myself and I blind myself to the truth.

V

The Resistant Way and Others

❖

Alienation

When I am resistant, it is as though I live by myself in a
psychological box.

Preoccupied with myself, I am divorced from others.

Surrounded by those I have rendered objects, I am surrounded,
but alone.

—⁓—

Whatever my outward show, below the surface I am insecure,
anxious, self-worried, defensive.

—⁓—

The resistant life is a life of alienation.

❖

PROVOCATION

When I feel alienated, I carry an attitude of blame toward others.

Feel blame, and I communicate blame. My words, my silence,
my expressions—all blame when I blame.

—⚶—

But people don't generally feel blameworthy.

Feeling my blame, they feel *unjustly* blamed.

My blame therefore invites others to betray themselves and
take offense.

My blaming of others invites their blaming of me.

My self-betrayal is provocational.

—⚶—

Likewise theirs.

Feeling justified in my blaming of them, I see their blaming of me
as unjustified and blame them all the more.

Self-betrayal provokes self-betrayal.

❖

Mutual Self-Betrayal

When others and I betray ourselves toward each other,
we cooperate in perpetuating each other's self-betrayals.

—ɷ—

Example:

Betraying myself toward another, I may feel unappreciated and
overwhelmed and see the other as unreasonably demanding.

I will feel compelled to resist the demands that are made of me.

If the other betrays herself in response, she is likely to feel
unappreciated and overwhelmed and see me as lazy
and unmotivated.

She will feel compelled to demand *more* of me.

—ɷ—

So the more I hold back, the more the other demands, and the
more the other demands, the more I hold back.

—ɷ—

Another example:

Betraying myself toward another, I may feel threatened and see the
other as self-interested and out to make me look bad.

I will feel compelled to withhold information and push my
objectives in a high-profile way.

If the other betrays himself in response, he is likely to feel
threatened by what he sees as *my* self-interestedness.

He will feel compelled to withhold information and push *his own*
objectives in a high-profile way.

So the more I hoard information and push for attention, the more
the other does the same, and the more the other does the same,
the more I feel I must hoard and push.

—⚋—

Consider the insanity:

Betraying myself, I invite in others the very behavior I say
I hate in them.

And betraying themselves, they invite the very behavior they say
they hate in me.

We cooperate in condemning ourselves to ongoing misery and woe.

❖

PROOF AND JUSTIFICATION

But in such insanity I find advantage:

When others and I betray ourselves toward each other, we provide
each other with what we most desire—justification.

—∞—

Ask me, when I am betraying myself, what I want most. I will say:

"I wish those people would stop."
"I wish they would change."
"I wish they would cooperate."

—∞—

But is this the full truth?

Why then do I act in a way that invites them to do the opposite?

And why, when they do change, do I refuse to accept the
change graciously? Why do I say:

"It's about time."
"It's too little."
"They don't really mean it."
"What are they up to?"

—∞—

The reason:

As long as I am blaming, I need others to be blameworthy so that
I will be justified in blaming them.

—⚹—

Others' mistreatment of me is proof of their blameworthiness.
And my mistreatment of them is proof of mine.

So when others and I betray ourselves toward each other,
we "collude" in providing each other with justification.

It is as if we enter an illicit agreement:

"I'll mistreat you so you can blame your bad behavior on me,
if you'll mistreat me so I can blame my bad behavior on you."

—⚹—

Our mutual mistreatment makes possible our mutual
self-justification.

❖

Mistreatment and Suffering

However bitterly I complain about others' mistreatment
of me, and of the suffering it has caused me, I also find it
strangely *delicious:*

It is my proof that others are as blameworthy as I have claimed
them to be.

And that I am therefore as innocent as I claim myself to be.

—∞—

I don't like suffering, but I like the innocence I find
in suffering.

—∞—

So I come to prize my suffering. And I sustain it by refusing
to forgive.

My wrong, then, is double.

Sustain my suffering and I embrace it.

Embrace my suffering and I embrace the mistreatment that
occasioned it.

—∞—

So what I say I hate, I embrace.

What I say I wish would die, I keep alive.

The justification I derive from this, though bought at the price of deep suffering and anguish, is nevertheless delicious.

—⁓—

In my resistant, alienated way of being, I am unhappy, insecure, and alone.

But at least I know I am justified.

❖

Bonds of Anguish

Although I feel alone, my blaming of others and their blaming of
me creates a bond between us:

We share the blame, pain, and suffering that we have created
together in our mutual self-betrayal.

—∞—

The suffering we experience is created and suffered *together*.

—∞—

The bonds that unite us are bonds of anguish.

VI

No Resistant Way to Responsiveness

❖

Behavioral Styles

Resisting others, I may exhibit many different behavioral styles
toward them.

—⚄—

I may explode, berating them for the obstructions they
are in my life.

I may control my temper, self-righteously displaying my virtue in
not berating them for the obstructions they are in my life.

I may indulge and drown them in sweetness, manipulating them
for the purposes they may serve in my life.

I may ignore and disdain them, noting only the insignificance
they are in my life.

I may blame myself, hating the desperate shambles that my parents
and others have made of my life.

And so on.

—⚄—

On the surface, these various resistant styles may seem
very different.

But the difference is illusion:

Each of them flows from the resistant way of being. In each of
them, I blame. In each of them, I see others as objects. In each,
I carry an attitude of justification.

—m—

Below the surface, at their core, all resistant behavioral styles are
the same.

They flow from self-betrayal.

❖

False Change

Within my resistant way of being toward others, I cannot
conceive of genuine change.

—∞—

I may shift from displaying my temper to controlling it.

I may shift from hating people to ignoring them.

I may shift from exalting myself to hating myself.

—∞—

In each case, I change. But only outwardly. Inwardly, there has
been no change at all.

Every resistant change is a change merely in my style
of resistance.

—∞—

But in my resistant way of being, that is all that change can
mean to me.

I cannot give up seeing others as the problem because from my
perspective I am convinced *they cause me* to see them as
the problem.

So part of *having* my deep attitude of blame is believing

that I can't change it.

—⁓—

Betray myself and my blaming attitude guarantees that any change I think of will continue to carry the same blaming attitude.

It guarantees that any change I think of will only be a change in style.

—⁓—

In self-betrayal, the lie I am living perpetuates itself.

❖

Is Change Possible?

I confront the difficulty of effecting genuine change as
I ponder the following questions.

—◊◊—

What kind of thoughts am I having when I am betraying
myself—when I am in the resistant way of being?

Resistant thoughts.

—◊◊—

What kind of thoughts *can* I have as long as I am betraying myself
and in the resistant way of being?

Resistant thoughts.

—◊◊—

As long as I am betraying myself and in the resistant way of being,
can I have any resistant thoughts that will lead me to stop
being resistant?

No.

—◊◊—

So how can I change? How can I pass from the resistant way of
being to the responsive?

Indeed, is such change possible at all?

VII

Becoming Responsive

❖

THE NATURE OF CHANGE

Anything I can think of while I am being resistant will itself
be resistant.

This means that while I am in the resistant way of being,
I cannot *will* a change to the responsive way of being.

—⚏—

Nothing I can do *within* my resistant way of being can bring
about a change *of* that way of being.

Trying to change myself by thinking of myself is futile.

—⚏—

So, is change, then, futile?

No. Just different than supposed.

—⚏—

The key to understanding:

Changing myself requires something outside myself.

—⚏—

That something is always present in the form of other people.

Other people's reality constantly beckons me, and it is that reality
that I have been resisting.

I can cease resisting.

—⁂—

So I don't change by trying to change myself—by trying to *make* myself responsive.

(After all, who am I thinking of when I am trying to change myself?)

I change by forgetting myself in response to others— by being attentive to and concerned about their needs, concerns, and objectives.

—⁂—

This very response is the change from the resistant to the responsive way of being.

❖

LIBERATION QUESTION 1

How can I begin to forget myself in response to others?

—⚭—

Betraying myself, I display several elements of
self-justification:

I blame with words—with what I think.

I blame with emotions—with how I feel.

I feel victimized by those I blame.

I horribilize those I blame.

I distort and exaggerate values that justify me against those
I blame.

I insist on my virtue.

I construct images of myself—images that turn others into
objects of blame.

—⚭—

As I ponder my life I can ask this question:

Do I show any of these signs of self-betrayal toward others?

—⚬—

To sincerely question my own virtue is to consider whether my self-justifications may be false.

—⚬—

In my question lies my liberation.

❖

LIBERATION QUESTION 2

Betraying myself, I feel innocent and justified in my
own behavior.

I am living a lie that I have done no wrong and that others
are at fault.

—⁓—

In order to escape this lie, I can ponder a second question:

What is the full truth about myself toward others?

Am I as innocent as I think I am?
Am I as justified as I insist I am?
Is there any place I've done wrong?

—⁓—

To ask this question is to challenge my lie.

To challenge my lie is to dispel it.

—⁓—

In the dispelling of my lie lies my liberation.

❖

LIBERATION QUESTION 3

Betraying myself, I see others as monstrous.

I see them as mistreating, abusing, injuring, or provoking me.

—∿—

In order to see more clearly, I can ponder a third question:

What is the full truth about those I am blaming?

Are they as monstrous as I think?
Are they as guilty as I insist?
Is there really no virtue in them?
Is there no room for compassion?

—∿—

To ask these questions is to ask what burdens others
may carry.

To ask what burdens others may carry is to begin
seeing them as people.

—∿—

In the seeing of others as people lies my liberation.

❖

LIBERATION QUESTION 4

Being resistant, I am betraying myself.

Betraying myself, I am resisting what I feel is right, *right now.*

—◊◊◊—

In order to quit betraying myself, I can consider a fourth question:

What is the right thing to do toward others that I am resisting right now?

—◊◊◊—

To ask this question is to discover its answer.

—◊◊◊—

In the discovering and doing of the answer lies my liberation.

VIII

The Responsive Way

❖

Truth and Compassion

Cease betraying myself and I see that my pain, my anguish,
my irritation, my anger—all were self-inflicted.

I was the creator of victimization and blame.

—⚭—

If others are betraying themselves, they too create
their misery.

Nevertheless, I have helped them do it. I have collaborated with
them in the proliferation of shared anguish.

—⚭—

When I see the truth, I feel care and compassion.

❖

ACTION

Feeling care and compassion, I have recovered my sense of
what others need.

—∽—

I see things I can *do.*

Things I *should* do.

Things I *want* to do.

—∽—

Feel what I should do and betray it, and I wander again
in darkness.

Feel what I should do and do it, and I continue to walk
in light.

❖

THE RESPONSIVE EXPERIENCE

What does the responsive way feel like?

You know.

—ɯ—

Hold a child close who has skinned a knee.

Embrace your spouse before leaving on business.

Realize a wrong and apologize.

Suffer a wrong and don't require apology.

Care about another's needs.

Weep in gratitude.

Cry for another's pain.

Help until you want to help.

Visit someone in need.

Call Mom just to talk.

Correct a child with love.

Have excuse, and fail to see it.

See opportunity to slack off, and work harder still.

Be slighted, and not take offense.

See in him who serves, a person to be served.

❖

DISCOVERY

When I cease resisting others, I cease seeing them as potential reinforcements of, or threats to, my portrayal of myself.

I cease seeing them as an audience.

—⚬—

To abandon this view of them is to abandon the corresponding view of myself. Gone is self-preoccupation with "I am the sort of person who . . ."

I cease seeing myself as a performer.

—⚬—

Finally responsive to others, I find them.

And this I learn in doing so:

To seek myself is to find someone false.

To lose myself with others is to find someone true.

—⚬—

The only life to be found is the life I lose with others.

—⚬—

In the losing of my life is its finding.

❖

Recovery

In this finding, I have found a new way of being a person—
both with myself and with others.

—⁂—

My resistant, self-justifying way of being is changed into a way
that is open, serene, and joyfully responsive.

I am transformed.

—⁂—

I am transformed as I trade the *false* self of my self-betrayal for the
genuine self that I betrayed.

—⁂—

So I do not *create* the responsive way of being so much as
I *recapture* it.

I am recovered.

—⁂—

Genuine psychological liberation is the recovery, at last,
of who I really am.

❖

Transformation

This recovery changes everything.

No longer justifying myself in the present, my perceptions of
past and future change.

—⁓—

The father who was never there for me,

the sister who was always cruel to me,

the boss who demanded too much of me,

the child who disrespected me . . . .

Free now of self-justification, straightforward perception
replaces self-justifying perception. I am free to remember:

Playing catch with my dad,

laughing with my sister,

learning from my boss,

being offered the hand of my child . . . .

—⚭—

The life I have lived now seems new to me.

The people I have shunned now arouse concern in me.

Things I never would have considered doing for them,
now seem obvious to me.

—⚭—

Change in the present, and my views of past and future change in
the same instant. I am transformed.

To those I blamed yesterday, I offer a better today and tomorrow.

❖

HELPING OTHERS CHANGE

When I change, I give others a different person to respond to.

Give them a different person to respond to and I change
their world.

—∞—

I no longer exaggerate their faults and my virtue.

I no longer ignore their virtues and my faults.

I no longer use values to devalue them.

They are no longer objects of blame.

—∞—

Ceasing to resist them, I no longer provoke their resistance of me.

—∞—

This is the source of my greatest contribution.

Nothing I can do will help others cease their self-betrayals as much
as simply ceasing my own.

❖

EXPECTATIONS

"Others may not change when you change."

True.

—⚮—

But in the responsive way of being I am not offended
when they don't.

I am ceasing to blame others because it is the right thing to do for
them, not because of what I want them to do for me.

—⚮—

Expect others to change because *I* have changed, and I have not
changed as much as I think.

I have just found a new way to blame.

—⚮—

In the responsive way of being, my expectations are colored not by
accusation, but by compassion.

I understand that others carry burdens I do not see—
including burdens I have placed on them by my own prior
self-betrayals.

I accept this with equanimity.

—ᴪ—

Seeing now with compassion, my view of others changes whether
they change or not.

❖

Forgiveness

I may be a true victim. I may have been hurt and mistreated
by others.

—⁊⁊—

If I remain free from self-betrayal in those situations, however,
I won't additionally victimize *myself.*

A sense of genuine loss may continue, including feelings of sorrow
and grief. But I will not be burdened by the all-consuming quest to
blame and to insist on my own victimization.

My feelings may be sad, even grief-stricken, but they won't be
self-justifying.

—⁊⁊—

Free of self-betrayal, I will have no personal need for victimhood.

Needing no justification, I will find no advantage in others taking
advantage of me. I will derive no benefit from being mistreated.

I will suffer abuse less because I prize it less.

And I will find the capacity to forgive.

IX

Paths in Psychology

❖

The Psychodynamic Tradition

The claim of one view of human nature:

Part of our nature is irrational, aggressive, and primitive. This primitive,
negative impulse is fundamentally who we are.

We must mobilize other parts of our nature (such as our rationality
and our sense of ethics) in an effort to control this impulse. We are
condemned to war with ourselves.

—⚬—

But why should we think this? Why should we believe negative
impulses are fundamental to us?

What is called our deep, primitive "nature" is merely what we
experience when we betray ourselves. It is what we experience
when we are in the resistant way of being.

—⚬—

Experiences labeled as evidence of "primitive impulse" prove not
our nature, but the nature and ubiquity of self-betrayal.

Our negative impulse is less an expression of who we are than an
expression of *resistance* to who we are.

It is a falsification.

❖

Behaviorism

The claim of another view of human nature:

Beyond factors of genetic predisposition, human behavior is a function of external influences.

We are not, in a real sense, free. We imitate the conduct of others and are otherwise conditioned to behave according to the patterns of reinforcement and punishment we encounter.

Emotional difficulties of one sort or another bespeak an unfortunate reinforcement history.

I am a victim.

—⚮—

But can I be purely a victim when I am *presenting* myself
as a victim?

Presenting myself as a victim is precisely what I do when I betray
myself—when I am angry, resentful, self-pitying, indifferent.

—⚮—

In significant and profound ways, *I* create my emotional
difficulties. They are the way I assign blame to others
and innocence to myself.

I am free in ways that my blame denies.

The assertion of my victimhood is a lie.

—⟋⟍—

Those who believe my tale of victimhood fail to see my lie.

❖

HUMANISM

The claim of another view of human nature:

Psychological well-being consists in the development of the self.

This development requires the fulfillment of various needs—from the need for physical security, to the need for belonging, to the need for self-esteem, to the need for self-actualization, and so on.

Fulfilling my needs and developing my full potential requires authenticity.

*I am to be honest about my feelings; I am to "own" them;
I am to act congruently with them.*

*Authenticity toward my feelings is the key to psychological growth;
inauthenticity is the key to psychological stagnation and ill health.*

—᙭—

But what feelings am I to "own"?

When I feel resentful toward others, I think it's because of what *they* did to *me*. The truth, however, is that I am feeling resentful because of what *I* am doing to *them*.

What sense does it make to say that I ought to be honest about this feeling when *the feeling itself is misleading me?*

Is *this* authenticity?

Is *this* congruence?

Is this brand of honesty the precondition for my
psychological health?

—⚭—

Authenticity:

It is not a condition of honesty *about* my feelings, it is a
condition of honesty *in* my feelings.

—⚭—

Betray myself and the only authenticity I can achieve is of
the first sort. It is a false authenticity.

It is an elaboration of my lie.

❖

COGNITIVE THEORY

The claim of another view of human nature:

Feelings are based on thoughts. Thus, how we feel will depend on how we think.

Emotional difficulties arise from negative interpretations we attach to events. Change our thoughts—change what we tell ourselves— and we change our feelings.

—⁓—

But what kind of change does this view allow? How deep is the change it envisions?

—⁓—

The change I want: The change to responsiveness.

Cognitive theory would say: *"Think a new thought."*

—⁓—

The problem:

When I am resisting, I am blaming.

When I am blaming, the thoughts I can think are blaming.

Think a blaming thought and I still *feel* blaming.

—⁓—

If change depends on thoughts, then I can't change from blame to responsiveness. I may be able to choose a new *style* of blame, but the predicament of blame remains.

I am stuck.

—⁓—

But I am not stuck, for we all change.

And this we learn from the change:

I change from resistance not by trying to change myself (even by trying to change my thoughts), but by being alive to others—to their needs, their challenges, their hopes, their fears.

I forget my false self-justifying self when I begin really caring about others.

I change because of my responsiveness to others.

—⁓—

The change that really matters *precedes* a change in thoughts.

X

Choice

❖

FALSE RESPONSIBILITY

My choice in every moment amounts to a choice between the need to be justified and the desire to be responsible. I can't be both.

—⁓—

Ironically, when I choose justification, I often do so in the name of responsibility.

"Others are responsible for making my life more difficult," I say.

"Others are responsible for making me feel bad."

"Others are responsible for the difficulty they are having with me."

"Others are responsible for the feelings that trouble them about me."

—⁓—

I believe in and preach responsibility for the whole world, except me.

I live on an island called excuse, marooned by the justifications that I call responsibility.

This choice between responsibility and justification changes my view of freedom, as well.

Choose justification, and I believe in freedom for all but me.

I purchase my innocence in exchange for a prison.

❖

The Nature of Freedom

Some say: *"There is no freedom. My subjective experience of freedom is an illusion."*

Others say: *"There is freedom. Between stimulus and response lies a moment of choice. I choose my response."*

—∞—

The truth:

I am free, but my freedom lies deeper than I imagine.

I choose my way of being.

—∞—

Before I betray myself, I see others as people—people as real as I am.

Betraying myself, I see others resistantly, as objects.

The stimuli in my environment have changed. But it is not they who have changed; it is I.

—∞—

Honor my responsiveness toward others and I see them one way; betray that responsiveness and I see them another way.

So I do more than choose my response to the stimuli in my environment.

In choosing my way of being, I also choose the stimuli.

—∿—

Herein lies my freedom: The world I encounter springs from my own soul.

Herein lies my fate: Which world will spring from me?

❖

Hope

If others are responsible for my misery, I am stuck.

If I am responsible, I am free.

—✠—

Relieve me of responsibility and you think you do me a favor.

But your relief is condemnation.

—✠—

Without the power to choose misery, I lack the power to choose happiness.

—✠—

Only those who leave me without excuse are my friends.

Only they speak the truth.

Only they believe in me.

Only they offer hope.

—✠—

The power to choose is within me.

I choose every minute, every day.

Do I choose responsiveness, or resistance?

—ᴡ—

Choose resistance and I am blind to the choice.

Nevertheless I choose.

—ᴡ—

Therein lies my hope.

❖

About The Arbinger Institute

Arbinger was founded in 1979 to translate the self-deception solution into practical effect for individuals and organizations worldwide.

Since then, Arbinger has worked with thousands of individuals and organizations to transform performance.

Arbinger is recognized as a world leader in changing mindset to improve organizational culture and resolve conflict. Arbinger's clients range from individuals who are seeking help in their lives to many of the largest companies and governmental institutions in the world.

As an introduction to Arbinger's ideas, *The Choice* is rich with personal and organizational implications. If you are interested in learning about Arbinger's programs for individuals and organizations, please contact the Arbinger Institute.

The Arbinger Institute
Arbinger.com | 801.447.9244